If you're not playing the GAME, you're getting PLAYED by the GAME...

INTRODUCTION

Ladies, I know you want to meet Prince Charming and ride off into the sunset with him, have a few of his babies and live happily ever after. But the reality is, you're going to kiss a few frogs before you meet that prince. Yes, *Happily Ever After* will come for you at some point and you will get married to a wonderful man. But until that time comes, you've got to find a way to SURVIVE the jungle of THE DATING GAME...where lions, tigers and certified playas run wild!

You see, in the dating game you have hustlers and con artists, pimps and playas. You have wolves in sheep's clothing, and snakes in the grass.

And Honey Bee, YOU are a fish in that pool of sharks.

For every NICE GUY in the dating pool of eligible bachelors, there are a dozen bad boys looking to con their way into your panties, your bank account and your credit report.

Believe that!

In your quest to find *Mr. Right*, you will inevitably encounter a few dozen *Oh So Wrongs*.

And that's part of the game, part of life, something all women experience prior to meeting *The One*. The trick is not letting the manipulation, abuse and disloyalty of men who are playas –the type who use women up and spit them out- zap so much of your time and energy that you are too bitter or too broken to enjoy or appreciate a good man.

You see, *Mr. Wrong* aka *Playa, Playa* will sweet talk himself into your life and have you bending over backwards before you know it. His GAME is "get her and stick her"...up that is. He doesn't want you, only what you have to give him. And when he gets that thing (whatever that is), he's on to the next.

You can call him all you want and stalk his mother's house. You can cry and plead for answers, demand to know "why me?" *Playa, Playa* is gone, and you are left only with the gift of emotional scars.

Peep Game

A man who is a Playa is a master mind manipulator. He doesn't need you to give him the key to your heart, his GAME will break that mutha wide open.

Now, a smart woman chooses to learn how to spot a *Playa*, how to see their GAME coming a mile away. A smart woman wants to know what she's dealing with before she gives the pu$$y up or puts any money down.

Silly missies however, prefer the fantasy of lies men who are *Playas* tell. She doesn't want to see/hear the truth, and she pays dearly for that naivety. Man after man rules and regulates her love life. She gives, they take. And when one guy leaves…another picks up where he left off.

Smart or silly? You choose your position!

I always say, "Peep game or stay lost in it!"

Your job as a single woman in 2015 is to make it through the jungle—to survive the roller coaster ride that is DATING and get to the other side unscathed. And you want to arrive in style – fit and fly in your Louboutins looking like a star – without a Louis bag full of emotional baggage weighing you down.

When you do meet *The One* --your Prince Charming-- and he rides up on you in that chromed out Caddy, you want to be able to give him your heart, to open fully to the LOVE he is offering. You don't want fears and insecurities resulting from all the abuse you took from the men you dated between ages 16-25 to destroy the HAPPILY EVER AFTER relationship you've been dreaming about.

The only way *Miss Thing*, you are going to survive the dating game unscathed—without battle scars from years of emotional battles--is to learn how to PEEP GAME.

I am going to show you how to spot a *Playa*. I am going to help you avoid getting played!

I am going to reveal the 8 types of *Playas* that exist in the dating game. These are the lions, tigers and master manipulators you want to avoid. These are the wolves in sheep's clothing, and the snakes in the grass.

I am going to put you UP on all of their love games.

When you are done with this book, you will have the tools you need to protect your heart. And, as you meet men and date in the years to come, you can refer to this manual to stay ahead of the game.

Of course it will be up to you to heed the advice I'm giving you; but whenever you need it, whenever you THINK you might be dealing with a suspicious character, the information will be here.

All that said, let's get to the game!

WHAT IS A PLAYA?

A *Playa* is the guy who gets all the chicks. He has just enough swag, conversation, looks, money, etc. (or a combination of those qualities) to bait and ultimately GAME any woman he desires. He's living the life many guys dream about. He may have 99 problems, but getting laid ain't one.

Being the kind of guy who can get women with relative ease, *The Playa* believes all women are easy. His experience with women has taught him that a little conversation goes a long way.

He's not the kind of guy who will put a lot energy into a woman without her showing signs of weakness—weakness for him that is. Rather than waste time with a longshot, *The Playa* will almost always gun for a sure thing.

The Playa is used to having his way with women. He knows what women want to hear, need to hear—to turn up. Of course that means have sex...

He has developed strategies for getting women to talk about their innermost desires, to reveal their long-held dreams early on in the courtship. And this information he uses to RUN GAME on them.

"I really want to have children by 30" unsuspecting women reveal to The Playa.

"I've never had a man spoil me…" spill a few others.

The Playa is taking notes…

Knowing what a woman secretly wants and strongly desires is one of *The Playa's* biggest tricks. How else would he know what to say to his new flame to get her to open her legs? How else would he know which one of his personas to showcase and which script to run on her?

Conversation is key! *The Playa* appeals to his target woman's innermost desires and makes her believe HE is her dream come true.

"Romance and intimacy? Baby I got you" the Playa says!

"Money? I have that." "Whatever you need, I can get it or, I'll die trying. Anything for you Boo."

"I know you've been done wrong. I don't want to hurt you baby. I just want to love you better than any man ever has."

"I'm the one you've been looking for. Trust me. Open your heart to me" The Playa promises.

"Just open your ~~legs~~ heart," he charms "and everything will be alright."

Yeah, homeboy is smooth…but that's a *Playa* for you.

That said, let me give you the common characteristics of *Playas*. That way you can easily spot his slick ass when you come across him.

CHARACTERISTICS OF A PLAYA

ARROGANCE:

The Playa believes he's God's gift to women. He sees himself as a great catch and doesn't believe there are too many women who wouldn't jump at the chance to be with him. He also believes he's smarter than most women. He'll say things like, *"I'm going to take you to the best restaurant you've ever been to"* and *"That guy got hung up on you because he's soft."*

He has dealt with so many EASY women, he believes all women are easy.

If you try to correct *The Playa*, try to point out the flaws in his myopic thinking, he will most likely chuckle and change the subject or hit you with a comment like, *"Why are you trying so hard to figure me out? Let it flow mama!"*

In his mind, you are too slow to pick up on his script and are surely lost…in all of his good GAME.

ENTITLED:

Most men believe they have to do *something* to get *something* from a woman.

It may be small, but most guys know and understand that SOMEthing must be given for someTHING to be received.

That's not how *The Playa* thinks. *The Playa* feels entitled to pu$$y. Those other guys have to work for it, have to earn the cookie "I'm entitled to it" *The Playa* thinks. In his mind, *"As long as I show up, f*cking you is a guarantee!"*

"Dinner? That can wait…UNTIL after I get some pu$$y!"

"Conversation? *Let's talk AFTER we bone. I need to see if we have sexual chemistry!"*

"Security? Commitment? *Life is short. Let's not waste a moment! Just go with the flow BABY."*

The Playa doesn't subscribe to tradition, those old-fashioned ideas like,

- A man should court a woman before sexing her
- A man should invite a woman to dinner and offer to pay
- A man should not take a woman sexually unless he truly desires her companionship.

The Playa believes he is entitled to have **who** he wants and **what** he wants from a woman on G.P. - that's *General Principle* - aka por nada.

CHEAP:

IF *The Playa* asks you out on a date, he'll either select a freebie date like a walk along the beach, a cheap date like a neighborhood wine festival where it's only $20 to dine and wine or, he'll spend big money but you'll be expected to work off every dollar that night…and I mean, EVERY dollar.

The big spender type of Playa will let you know off top that you need to repay him. He'll say something like, *"Now I'm spending all of this money on you. What can you do for me?"*

CHARM:

Charm is disarming. Almost every woman can be wooed into a relationship with charm, and just as many women can be convinced to stay in a relationship because of a *Playa's* well-practiced charisma.

Playas are masters of charm. Instead of raising their voice when you get upset and responding in kind to your angry accusations and insults, a *Playa* will lower his voice. It's called flipping the script. He'll change the tempo and the direction of the argument by speaking softly and feigning concern.

"How can I change baby? What do I need to do to make you happy?"

The thing is, *The Playa* is not really looking to please you or satisfy you with calm words. No, *The Playa* just wants to change the subject. Whatever he needs to say or do to get you back ON THE BUS (as Reality TV star Stevie J is famous for saying) will be said and done.

SEXUAL SEDUCTION:

Sex is not only a tool *Playas* use to get women hooked on them, sex is a tool *Playas* use **to keep the woman they're dating sprung on them**…long after they've used and misused them to no end.

Men who are *Playas* often have their sex game on point. They know where to lick and how to stick their target woman so that she squeals with delight. Unlike the *Average Cat*, a *True Playa* is willing to go the extra mile sexually–which is useful both in baiting his catch AND keeping her on his hook.

The moment a woman shows signs of pulling away, of wising up to his bullsh*t, *The Playa* will demand that she see him.

He will thrust and lick his way back into her good graces leaving her in a haze of ecstasy. As she falls asleep dreaming of him…*Playa, Playa* heads off to his next exploit (that is, Girlfriend #2 or 3).

CROCODILE TEARS:

Crocodile tears are used most often when a *Playa* is confronted by a woman. *Playas* are masters of conjuring emotions so they can feign excitement AND sadness on a dime.

Often after being confronted by their target woman, a *Playa* will drop a few tears. Since *The Playa* is not usually emotional, his naive lover THINKS her Playboy is opening up and breaking down.

"He gets it" she thinks!

Not so! *The Playa* is manipulating his woman into thinking he cares when he could really give 2 flying f*cks.

All *The Playa* wants is his target's head back in his game so that he can continue to run game.

RIGHTEOUS INDIGNATION:

Another tactic *Playas* use when confronted by a woman for doing her wrong?

Righteous Indignation!

He'll rear up violently at any suggestion he has done something wrong. His response to a simple question like, *"Where have you been all night"* will be explosive and alarmingly aggressive.

"Are you crazy? What is wrong with you? Here I am trying to be good to you, and here you are tearing me down–accusing me of A, B, C!"

Yeah, that's *The Playa*. Like a rabbit in a hole, he's caught before the barrel of your gun. He's got one move left and that's intimidation.

Is he really upset? No, but by APPEARING upset, most women (including YOU) will back up and cower down.

EXPLOITATION OF POWER:

Playas are sometimes men in positions of control. Think Bill Clinton (and his string of secret mistresses). Think P.

Diddy (and his penchant for dating women younger/less powerful than him).

These men will purposefully date women who are beneath them socially, mentally, economically or, professionally so that they can exploit them. Their POWER becomes their CONTROL and LEVERAGE in the relationship.

This is often seen in workplaces when the boss chooses to sleep with one of his subordinates. The subordinate may fall in love or try to gain control in the relationship. That's when the boss will assert his POWER and put her back in her place.

When you see a man consistently seeking out women who are beneath him in some way…you have to ask yourself this question: *"Is he a Playa?"*

If so, the reasoning behind his dating strategy is CONTROL. Now you know!

Side Note: I have nothing against Diddy or President Clinton, but I've got to use somebody you know to make my points.

GAS LIGHTING:

Gas Lighting is an extremely effective strategy *Playas* use to confuse and manipulate women. In essence, they make women doubt what they see.

Here's an example of gas lighting:

PLAYA: *"Do you really think I would cheat on you? And with her?"*

WOMAN: *"But I saw you touch her butt. Didn't she slide you her number? I know what I saw."*

PLAYA: *"Baby, stop being so insecure. I can't believe you're letting that girl get to you. You are the baddest b*tch around. What would I want with her?"*

WOMAN: *"I know what I saw…"*

PLAYA: *"Listen, you think you saw something but it didn't happen. It wasn't real. What's gotten into you? What happened to the confident woman I met? Where is she? Huh? Look at me babe. You know I love you!"*

You know what you saw. You know what you heard, but *The Playa* will convince you that what you thought you saw or believed you heard was inaccurate. By the time

Playa, *Playa* spins his web of lies, you will be thoroughly confused about the reality of a situation.

The Playa doesn't need you to believe him 100%. He just needs to create enough doubt within your mind, that you drop the subject.

Now that I've given you the characteristics of a *Playa*, I'm now going to reveal the 8 types of Playas you will encounter most often in the dating game.

There is **The Buddy Playa**, **The Hard Luck Playa**, **The Religious Playa**, **The Playa Pimp**, **The Married Playa**, **The International Playa, The Jail Bird** and **The Web Browser**.

Peep Game!

THE HARD LUCK PLAYA

If you meet a man and he tells you a sob story of any kind (during the first few months of knowing you), watch out! These men are usually *Playas* and their game is the "Feel Sorry for Me/Give Me Some Money" Game.

The Hard Luck Playa is looking to gain sympathy as a means of opening you up to manipulation. He'll tell you a sob story hoping to get you invested in his drama.

Don't even be surprised if *The Hard Luck Playa* hits you up day one for some money.

You're sitting at dinner and he "forgot" to bring his high limit credit card.

"I got you he says. My treat next time."

You're disappointed and even suspicious but hey, maybe he really did forget his card.

Another angle of *The Hard Luck Playa* is spending a little money. He'll spend a few coins on a lovely romantic evening but at the end of the night he'll claim to need $10 for something or another. You give it to him thinking, *"Well, he just spent a grip on me--why not help him out?"*

Confused? Just remember one thing about *The Hard Luck Playa*. He will ask for money or a financial favor **soon after the two of you meet**.

He may even try to disguise his game plan by pretending he just wants a "small loan."

"Can I hold $20 until next week?"

He has a job. "I'm sure he'll pay me back" you think.

His first request will usually be for a small amount of money. This is how he tests the water…

After getting that small change, he'll go for the gold. He'll hit you up for a larger amount of money. He'll tell you some sob story about why he needs the money urgently. He will appeal to the nurturer in you, slyly placing you in the role of 'mother'. He will appeal to your desire to be a good woman.

His hard luck somehow becomes **your** problem to solve.

He will even make you feel good about helping him. He'll tell you how he's never had ANYONE support him. He'll claim you are his blessing, a Godsend.

He will claim there is no one else he can go to…

"Help me Baby," he pleads!

You think, *"He needs me. There is no one else. If the shoe was on the other foot, he'd do the same for me."*

Yeah right!

You give up the money.

You co-sign on an auto loan so that *Playboy* can get a new car for work.

You put an iPhone in your name so that he doesn't lose contact with his kids…

What a good ~~silly~~ woman you are!

Then…suddenly…the phone calls stop! You haven't talked to *Playa, Playa* in days.

You can't get the guy on the phone. You're leaving message after message but for some reason, your calls keep going to voicemail.

What's going on?

The very available guy you met a month ago is now responding to texts with emoticons and shorthand text messages like, "CYBL" (Call You Back Later).

WTF?

He's letting you down easy…trying ease you out of his life.

OR, his number changes. He seems to have moved. Someone you never heard of is now answering YOUR MAN'S phone.

What's going on?

I'll tell you. *Do you really want to know?*

YOU'VE BEEN PLAYED!

He's gone. *The Hard Luck Playa* has gotten what he wanted from you and now he is on to the next victim.

He will either disappear from your life completely or he will pop in and out so sporadically you won't know what to think.

That's game!

Peep Game

The Hard Luck Playa will not try to maintain contact with a woman after getting money from her UNLESS he believes he can trick her out of more cash down the line.

HOW CAN YOU SPOT THE HARD LUCK PLAYA?

- He will either ask for cash money or, he will ask for a financial favor like getting added to your phone plan or co-signing on a loan.

  "I need to stay with you for a few weeks until this or that comes through."

  "I have this line on a new job but its 50 miles from my home. If I had a car I could be making $25/hr. Can you loan me $2,500 for a down payment on a car? I could pay you _____ each pay period."

  "My cousin ran my phone bill up calling his girl. My phone is about to be cut off. I don't know what I'm going to do. I don't want to lose you because of this. (Hint, Hint)

- He will always have a sob story that makes him look like a victim.

  "My baby's mother is a b*tch. Ever since I stopped messing with her she's been stalking me. I have to get out of my apartment....but my credit isn't that

great. If I could move, I would feel more comfortable bringing you over."

*"I just lost my job. My boss had it in for me though. He didn't like me from the first day. I don't know why. Maybe it's because I'm young and good-looking. Yeah, I just got fired, I'm good though. I have some jobs lined up. I just need a little something to make rent **this month**."*

Every woman I have ever dated has been obsessed with money. I'm a good man so I give you know? Sometimes people take advantage of a good person. I have helped so many people—my family, my friends, even my ex-girlfriend's mom. I'm a giver. Now that I'm in a spot (financially), no one wants to help me!"

- He will almost always hit you up for money early in the courtship. He wants to gage your willingness to help him and your gullibility. If he sees that you are not a viable *Mark* (aka a gullible target), he will quickly end things with you and move on.

THE BOTTOM LINE

The Hard Luck Playa will want to use your credit card or your car. He will want cash money or to use a line of your credit. He will ask to stay with you (if he has nowhere else to go) or, he will ask you to put an apartment lease in your name. The thing you have to remember about *The Hard Luck Playa* is this: He's not into you…he's not after you…he is only interested in what you can and are willing TO GIVE him.

FLIPPING THE GAME

How do you flip the game on *The Hard Luck Playa*?

Offer nothing to a man up front! This is *Playa 101* for women. Let a man pay for dinner and the first…everything. It's not about showing your independence. In the early stages of a relationship, you need to gage where a man's head is. You need to know his angle BEFORE you start giving money to him. Besides, it's a man's nature to make the bacon and bring home the bread. Let him play his position.

The only men I've ever known to resist paying for dates or splurging on a woman they were interested in, were the men who had no money OR men who were planning to run the 'Hard Luck Game'.

If you do things this way and you find out a guy's a Hard Luck Playboy…at least you got a few free meals for your time and energy.

THE BUDDY PLAYA

The Buddy Playa is a man who poses as a friend in order to gain access to his target and glean information about her. The goal of *The Buddy Playa* is to work his way into a woman's head and game her (over time) into f*cking him.

<u>Peep Game</u>

The Buddy Playa poses as a friend but he's really just a cleverly disguised spy.

He wants to know your likes and dislikes, your weaknesses and character flaws. He wants to

know who you are dating and when you got dumped. He wants to know what makes you smile and who/what makes you wet.

This guy is someone you probably don't find attractive. He's not your type.

He may have approached you for a date but you quickly friend zoned him. Instead of slinking away, this master playa found another way in.

He's playing the role of friend…gathering information about you that he can use to manipulate you later. He'll wait around for the right time and STEP TO YOU.

You think you've met a great new friend! The Buddy Playa…

- Compliments you often, which makes you feel good
- He calls you a lot, and seems to care what's going on in your life.
- He always say how much he appreciates your friendship, how good a woman you are.

Great right? What a pal he is!

No! *The Buddy Playa* is setting you up for the kill. He's doing nothing but running game. He's prepping you for

Act II. He softening you up, opening you up…get it? You'll see in time just how slick this guy really is.

All of his 'nice' gestures are nothing more than illusions. *The Buddy Playa* is pretending to be your *B.F.F* but he's really priming you to be *D.T.F* aka *Down to F*ck*.

And he'll wait as long as it takes to get you OPEN. He'll bide this time talking on the phone with you, visiting with you, and watching movies with you and the girls.

He may even take you out to dinner, treat you to a day at the spa or, buy you an expensive birthday gift.

Pay attention girlfriend! This is how the game is played!!!

There is no rush to get you in bed. *The Buddy Playa* is the type who enjoys a long chase. He loves a woman who challenges him. He lives to FLIP situations in his favor. That's his kick – winning women over, convincing them over time that he is a good man.

He knows you will cave...eventually. He knows at some point you will let him in. That's the day *The Buddy Playa* is waiting for. That is the day he will FLIP THE GAME on you. That is the day he will get what he wanted from you since *Day One*.

Until THAT DAY, he will work you. He will…

- Bash every guy you date, calling them unworthy of you.
- Claim the guy you met at Starbucks is a *Playa* and the guy you met at the grocery store is secretly married.
- Confound and confuse you with contradicting advice about men.

Before long you will not trust any guy—only your tried and true *BFF*.

And that's just the way *The Buddy Playa* wants it. He wants…needs you to trust him and everything that HE SAYS about men.

Outside of knowing a person's emotional drives and triggers, trust and comfort are the two things a *Playa* needs in order to run game on a person.

The Playa wants to be the one you trust and the one you open up to.

Peep Game

How many guys have you befriended only to wind up dating months or years later?

The Buddy Playa gets close to a woman by posing as her friend. He takes note of her habits, her likes and dislikes, her insecurities and her dating experiences.

This is the information he will use against her.

He will work himself into her mind, into her thoughts and eventually into her bed. Overtime, HE will become her main man!

What happens when a woman has sex with the *The Buddy Playa*? He disconnects!

That's what *Playas* do.

When you do give *The Buddy Playa* your heart or you break down and give him some pu$$y, he will turn on you. Two years of friendship, five years, ten? It doesn't matter.

The Buddy Playa has been working for THIS DAY. Beyond that…exists nothing at all.

I have seen *Buddy Playas* wait patiently to BREAK a woman and then cease all communication with her immediately after sleeping with her or getting her to fall in love.

Once the tide turns and *The Buddy Playa* is the one IN DEMAND, he is usually turned off. At that point, it's on to the next challenge.

HOW CAN YOU SPOT THE BUDDY PLAYA?

Let's review his characteristics:

- He will most often be a man you turned down for romance or a guy you put into the friend zone.

- He will (at first) appear unphased by you turning him down. He will instead begin to worship you as if you are the most beautiful woman in the world.
  "You are so beautiful."
  "I love your hair like that."

"You are the prettiest girl…"

- He will invite you out often and he will offer to pay. Ask yourself *"What's in it for him?"*

- He will flirt with you often but act like he's just joking around.
  "I know you don't want me. I'm just playing with you."

- He will knock every guy you meet/date. I repeat, HE WILL KNOCK EVERY GUY YOU MEET/DATE!!!

Like my *Playa Partna* often says…*The Buddy Playa* is waiting at the back door for his opportunity to get inside.

Peep Game!

THE BOTTOM LINE

In most cases *The Buddy Playa* will ease his way out of your everyday life. He no longer needs to keep tabs on you. He no longer needs to work you…so he oftentimes will want to create distance between the two of you.

How will he slither out of the friendship? With a clever lie of course. Something like the following will be used to EXPLAIN why he can no longer visit for hours or chat into the late night hours…

- *"I just got back with _____. You know how jealous she is. I'm just trying to keep things cool. You understand don't you?"*

(Ex-girlfriends and baby mommas are commonly used as buffers. They may rarely be spoken of until *The Playa* needs an excuse to disappear. All of a sudden it's all about what she wants).

- *"I know I haven't called but work has been crazy. My boss has me overloaded. As soon as things ease up, we'll catch up. Let's go to _____. My treat."*

(*The Buddy Playa* has assumed the lead/power role in the relationship. He is now dictating WHEN you see him and for how long. This shift in power and control is what *Playas* call 'flipping the game').

- *"I made a goal to get my body in top form by the summer. I'm working out 5 days a week after work now. It's rough,, but the payoff will be worth all of this effort."*

(Playboy just eliminated most of his free time in one swoop. He knows there is little anyone will say about a person who is trying to get healthier or in better shape. Exercise is an easy out for *Playas* that few women ever question).

- *"Man, all of a sudden you're so clingy. I didn't know this about you. I thought we trusted each other."*

(*The Buddy Playa* makes you out to be insecure and clingy. Most women hate those labels and will start acting super nonchalant and independent in order to convince a man that they ARE NOT insecure and clingy. Here's the trick though. You are doing exactly what *The Buddy Playa* wants you to do -- giving him space and time)

- *"I didn't expect all of this to happen. I don't know how I feel. I don't want to move too fast."*

(*The Buddy Playa* is slowing down the pace of the relationship and moving YOU into the friend zone. Once again, he has flipped the game).

It's all about manipulation and control for *The Buddy Playa*. First, he learns everything about you…then he uses what he knows to PLAY YOU. By the time you fall for this Playboy, he's 9 miles into the next chick.

FLIPPING THE GAME

How do you flip the game on *The Buddy Playa*?

Resist making close friendships with men. I know that sounds harsh, but I'm talking about making heterosexual men your *BFF*.

Have male friends. Talk to them. Go out with them. Party with them. But under no circumstances do you tell these guys your secrets, details about your relationships with other men, sex life or, about any of your insecurities.

If a *Playa* has little or no information to work with, it is virtually impossible for him to manipulate you!

Remember, *The Buddy Playa* appears to be a good friend but in reality, he is trying to glean usable information.

THE RELIGIOUS PLAYA

The Religious Playa is a difficult *Playa* to spot. Rarely do we question people who are religious or spiritual. But that's the beauty of this playboy's disguise! No one is looking beyond his chaste exterior. There is no better example however, of a wolf in sheep's clothing.

The Religious Playa uses a woman's devotion to God to get her open, comfortable and stuck on stupid. He works his way into her mind quoting Bible scriptures and well-known wisdoms. Once she's primed, he'll take everything she's willing to give including sex and money.

When *The Religious Playa* goes to church on Sunday mornings, he's not there just to hear the Word. He is hunting for his next big fish.

HOW CAN YOU SPOT THE RELIGIOUS PLAYA?

- The moment you meet this guy, *The Religious Playa* will reference God/religion. He wants to gage your response. He wants to know if you are the type of woman he can manipulate and play.

  He may say something to you like, *"God is good isn't He?"*

- He'll saturate you with quotes from and interpretations of the Word. He'll pepper your conversation with him with Bible references.

- He'll make sure you know that he attends church— that he is a good Christian. He may even invite you to a service.

- As your relationship develops *The Religious Playa* will start using God to control you. He will say you are *"too worldly"* and need to go out less. He may say you dress too provocative, and *"need to please God"* and *"cover up."* He may even say God told him to tell you X, Y and Z.

Many women will listen to this advice from *The Religious Playa,* not because they are dumb, but because they really want to please God, and believe the person advising them is a man of God. They may start going to parties less and may start dressing more conservatively.

This is what I call master manipulation.

Peep Game

A master CON MAN will use something a person already believes in strongly (like religion) to persuade them to act a certain way or, to do a certain thing.

Control is the first step for *The Religious Playa*. He wants a woman to **LISTEN** to him, **BELIEVE** what he says, and **FOLLOW** his instructions. If *The Religious Playa* can get his target woman to **LISTEN**, **BELIEVE** and **FOLLOW**, *he* knows he has a viable mark. He will then move to phase two of his manipulative game plan.

In the second phase of *The Religious Playa's* game, he uses a woman's devotion to God to get her to give him things.

"God wants you to help me!"

"God is going to bless you through me!"

"God told me WE are blessed as a unit! What WE have together, nobody can stop!"

"God sent me to you!"

"God told me you are the one!"

If money is what *The Religious Playa* is after, he'll hit his target up for a donation. He will claim he needs the money to do something righteous like pay overdue child support, start a business or invest in new vehicle for work. He will link his need to some kind of good cause and convince her that GOD WANTS <u>HER</u> TO BE HIS SUPPLY.

If she hesitates or refuses to comply, he'll insist her faith in God is weak.

My friend's mother fell for a *Religious Playa*! He moved into her home and stayed there rent free for over a year. He even set up a church in her basement. Get this though! *Playa, Playa* required my friend's mother to pay a donation every Sunday just like the other parishioners even though he was living in her house for free. Before it was all over, dude put mama in the hole a few thousand dollars plus he ran up phone bills and other expenses. When mama started seeing through Playboy's game, dude moved out suddenly and presumably on to the next *Trick*.

Money is usually what *The Religious Playa* is after. But not always. Sometimes religious playboys want easy sexy not money.

In those situations, *The Religious Playa* will use God and religious commandments to control and manipulate his target.

He will talk incessantly about the importance of virtue. He will claim that the woman he settles down with not only has to be a good woman…but a virtuous woman. He will use scripture to confirm his stance on sex and dating, and he will emphasize what the Word says about a loose woman.

This is the control part of his game! *The Religious Playa* can't risk losing his target to another man so he MENTALLY LOCKS HER DOWN with religious rhetoric. Then, when he's sure she is locked in -- sitting at home waiting on him every night -- he'll seduce her sexually.

At this point, the target now feels completely devoted to *The Playa*. He has her mind and her body under his control.

SIDE NOTE: Yes, *The Religious Playa* is contradicting himself – preaching one thing but doing another – but at this point, his target is too sprung to notice.

THE BOTTOM LINE

The Religious Playa's goal is to control how you think and how you see the world. He wants you to believe in and follow him.

His religious talk is nothing more than a line – a well-crafted script. It's a con -- his way of softening women up and getting them open.

When *The Religious Playa* gets what he wants from a woman, he will move on. And, he'll leave her life the same way he came in… praising the Lord!

Peep Game

*Some Religious Playas are in fact ministers.
These men will have their wife in the first pew
and their mistresses littered about the
congregation.*

*They use the Word of God to control and
manipulate each woman. When they are done
using a woman for sex/money…they will use that
same Word to denounce and destroy her. In this
way, they get rid of threats to their operation.*

MORE SIGNS YOU ARE DATING A RELIGIOUS PLAYA:

- He condemns your friends or certain aspects of your lifestyle.
- He backs everything he says (about you) up with references to the Bible or another religious doctrine.

- He insists you aren't living in accordance with God's Word and he claims to know what you need to do to get right with God.
- He blames every relationship problem and even every day challenges on <u>YOUR</u> lack of faith or spiritual missteps.
- He doesn't want to meet with a therapist or counselor to fix anything about himself or the relationship (even if he is abusive or has an addiction). He insists he doesn't need help…you do.
- He refers to you as a demon or a heathen.
- Despite encouraging you to meditate or pray daily, he rarely prays or meditates.
- He says he knows what God wants you to do.
- Despite putting up a front of praying and meditating in the beginning of the relationship -AND THIS IS KEY- his life won't reflect any evidence of prayer. He's broke. He has little/no relationship with his family. He's unemployed. He needs to borrow your car. Get it???

FLIPPING THE GAME

How do you flip the game on *The Religious Playa*?

Be wary of men who offer you advice about how to live days/weeks after meeting you. These types are usually looking for a mind to manipulate. Don't let that mind be yours.

If a guy insists on teaching you something about the Word, tell him your pastor gives you all the advice and encouragement you need.

"Thanks but no thanks Playa."

THE PLAYA PIMP

A pimp is a *Playa*. The only real difference between a *Playa* and a pimp is their end game.

A *Playa* enjoys charming, seducing and running game on women. His goal (typically) is to get as much pu$$y as he can get. A pimp on the other hand, wants to make money from the women he 'dates'. Sex is not important to him.

He charms, seduces and runs game on women for the purpose of turning them into bankable hoes.

The pimp's goal is to have as many women as possible financing his lifestyle. He plays the role of supervisor or talent manager to a stable of women who work (the track) and bring *Daddy* home their hard-earned money.

Most women will never meet an old school pimp -- that is, a man who actually pimps women out for money -- but some of you will run across men with pimp-ish ways. These mack daddies aka *Playa Pimps* don't have hoes on the stroll in the traditional sense, but they do con women into working for them.

The Playa Pimp wants one woman to finance his lifestyle. He will expect this woman to turn tricks every now and then with his friends and to participate in threesomes with other women.

This is legitimate pimping!

A female with a 9-5 job is trained and gamed to suck and f*ck on the side. In this way, *The Playa Pimp* has the best of both worlds. His girl works a regular job and gets a legitimate paycheck, but she can also hustle up extra money for *Daddy* on the side.

One of my partnas is a *Playa Pimp*. I've watched him play this game for years with different women. He charms a chick, gets her to move him into her house, then he turns her out. He'll make her think he's into threesomes—that having a 3rd party in the bedroom is his kick.

Thinking she's pleasing her man, the unsuspecting female starts engaging in threesomes with some of her friends as well as his.

Little by little my friend gets his woman to do a little more sexually. Eventually, she's a certified freak. He then flips the game on her and starts making money off of her freaky ass.

As you can see, this *Playa* is a pro! His pimp-ish mentality is that of a professional pimp. He knocks hoes and gets money too. He just uses straight chicks who work 9-5's to get what he wants, not prostitutes.

For a price, he'll let other men and even women have sex with his woman. It's Pimp Game 101 without the hassles of street life and 5-0.

HOW CAN YOU SPOT THE PLAYA PIMP?

- He has no job and no legitimate job history.
- He seems turned-on when guys try to holla at you. He urges you to talk to/befriend these guys or, he says things like, "Get that money!"
- When you walk down the street, he walks slightly ahead of you and never wants to hold hands.
- He encourages or insists that you to walk on the street-side of the sidewalk while he walks on the inside. (That's street code. It means, "That's my hoe!")
- He openly flirts with your friends and tells you to deal with it. He says, *"Why do you care? You're my number 1."*
- He does not try to hide the fact that he's having sex with your friends. In fact, he asks you to join them.
- He's not satisfied that you're working a 9-5. He suggests you get a part-time gig or that you find a part-time hustle.
- He tells everybody you're his "Wife" but he refuses to marry you.

- He refers to you as 'B*tch' in everyday conversations. *"B*tch! Get my wallet! Where's my food, B*tch? Where have you been B*tch? Don't let me have to tell you again, B*tch!"*
- His friends are pimps.
- He refers to men who have traditional relationships (aka equal partnerships) with women as *"Squares"*.
- His friends don't look you in the face and only speak to you when your man directs them to.
- He tells you how much money you need to bring home each week for him to stay with you.
- He rarely or never has sexual intercourse with you. He prefers that you perform oral sex on him. That act is not reciprocated.
- He suggests you get into porn or exotic dancing. He may even set-up an audition for you with a local porn producer or at a local strip club.

- He may show up with a friend one night and tell you to go into the bedroom and please him. This encounter is not just for fun; the friend has paid or agreed to pay for sex with you.

- He may start charming and seducing one of your friends. He'll create jealousy and competition between the two of you. He'll have both of you giving him money.
- He'll expect a large portion of your paycheck. He will say he needs _____ amount of money in order to stick around.

THE BOTTOM LINE

Watch out for men who talk about taking you to the next level or who say you're pretty enough to do porn or strip. These men want to be your manager not just your man. They are *Playa Pimps* who are looking to turn out a new hoe.

FLIPPING THE GAME

How do you flip the game on *The Playa Pimp*?

I'll give it to you in the raw. The only way to flip the game on *The Playa Pimp* is to become his Bottom Woman aka his Bottom B*tch.

Turn *The Playa Pimp* out on another woman. Convince him to give you some of the money she pays him. In this way, you become a *Playa Pimp* by proxy. You've slyly gained leverage and control in the relationship.

Hey, it's a dirty game! Oftentimes, it's play OR BE PLAYED!!!

THE BROOKS BROTHER

A lot of women think they can spot a *Playa*, but they are looking in all the wrong places for all the wrong things.

Movies often depict *Playas* as being exotic looking or very attractive. Playboys are also commonly portrayed in film as slimy-looking older men with slicked back hair who wear polyester suits.

These images contribute to women getting played. You're looking for one thing – something you saw in a movie – when the reality is very different.

Believe it or not, *Playas* don't walk around with Gator shoes and candy-colored Zoot Suits looking like Jerome from *Martin*. And few *Playas* dress like or act like the Playboys depicted on the show "Jersey Shore."

Playas are average guys with exceptional conversation skills and understanding of women. Their outer appearance varies depending on their geographic location, occupation and economic status. That said, watch out for *The Playa* in the *Brooks Brothers* suit. That conservative dresser is playing women too.

HOW CAN YOU SPOT THE BROOKS BROTHER?

At first glance, *The Brooks Brother* looks like a great catch. He's well dressed, well spoken, gainfully employed and polite. But his stunning appearance is a façade. This Playboy uses a good guy image to hide his bad boy mentality. In this way, *The Brooks Brother* easily lures unsuspecting women into his web of lies, deceit and manipulation.

The Brooks Brother's appearance is nothing more than a well-executed marketing plan. Look beyond that COVER to FIND OUT who he really is.

The following list reveals common characteristics and patterns of *The Brooks Brother* Playboy:

- He has never had a long-term relationship.
- He has a string of angry exes.
- He has children by multiple women.
- His tires and windshield have been slashed more than once.
- He earns $35,000/year but he drives an $80,000 car.
- He isn't interested in your life, what you've been through or your story. Conversations with him center on him.
- He cuts conversations by phone short claiming he's not a phone person. During dinner dates, he seems distracted or like he's prepping his next line while you're talking.
- He doesn't let you choose the restaurant or what you eat for dinner. He steers you to places he

prefers to eat and tells you what entre you would enjoy.

- When other women are present, he drops your hand or gets quiet.
- He asks you to pay for dates or hints that most women he knows pay their own way.
- If you mention having a problem or are sick, he avoids you until the crisis is over.
- He tells you he doesn't celebrate commercial holidays like *Valentine's Day*, *Christmas* or *Sweetest Day* soon after meeting.
- You rarely can get him on the phone. He's always busy.
- He's always going out of town.
- He watches a lot of porn or goes to strip clubs more than once a week.

Peep Game

Looks can be deceiving. Remember this as you play the dating game. Appearances can mask a person's true character. Don't get so caught up looking at a man's shoes and watch that you forget to look for clues to his character.

We're an image obsessed culture. Thus, we assume people who look a certain way are a certain way. Con artists like Tim Dog (a rapper turned entrepreneur who conned one woman out of $30,000 and many others out of thousands), are the kind of *Playas* women don't suspect. Men like Tim Dog are *The Brooks Brothers* I'm warning you about.

These guys look right and sound right so women assume they must be alright.

But *Playas* are masters of deception. Often, the image they present is nothing more than a smoke screen. *The Brooks Brother* is no different. Don't let his conservative attire fool you. This straight-laced dude may appear classy and on the up and up…but his mindset and approach to women is slimier and grimier than most thugs.

I've personally met some thug types who I damn near ran from when I met them, who wound up looking-out for me in ways I can't begin to repay. And I've met some classy *Brooks Brothers* type men who were so gutter and so pimpish, if I saw them on the street today, I'd look the other way. These brothers looked good but their mentality was down in the gutter.

THE BOTTOM LINE

The Brooks Brother is a Playa with a great marketing plan.

This *Playa* uses a front to lure women in. He dresses and presents himself as a professional Cat. He looks good, he sounds good…but it's all an illusion. If you really listen to this guy, you will pick up on his game. You will see that he is nothing to hold on to.

Don't assume every man who dresses like a thug has a thug mentality, and don't assume every man in a *Brooks Brothers* suit is a quality dude.

Peep Game

Gorgeous Dre, a reformed pimp who starred in the documentary "American Pimp," recently spoke to college students about using a corporate image to bait women.

Dre said his corporate image (a conservative suit and tie) helped him to knock hoes and proved to be the perfect disguise for his inner thought process. He said everyday women fell for his square attire and his executive speak…and by the time they realized they were being laced with game…they were already smitten and hooked on him.

Dre says he dressed normally and spoke intelligently, which fooled women into trusting him.

He also insisted the media's portrayal of pimps and Playas sends young women right into the arms of con men.

The Brooks Brother will look good to you! He's the guy you'll want to take to office parties and introduce to the family. He's intelligent, well-spoken, well-dressed and well-versed on many subjects. But like a high-end escort, he only looks good from afar.

His credentials won't hold up under any real investigation.

His suit is borrowed. The car is a rental. His business is nothing more than a post office box. Everything you know about *The Brooks Brother* is an exaggeration or a complete lie.

With this *Playa*, what you see IS NOT what you will get.

Over time, *The Brooks Brother's* façade will fall apart. Illusions are tricky that way. His carefully crafted image will give way and you will see what this *Playa* is really all about.

- He didn't really graduate from Cornell. In fact he didn't even finish college.
- He doesn't own a condo on the lake. He's actually crashing at his brother's place.
- His business doesn't exist. No income collected or taxes paid. He just passes out business cards to make people think he has it going on.
- He has 4 children, not just the cute little boy on his nightstand…but the mothers of those children are so fed up with *The Brooks Brother* that they don't bother to keep in touch.

The Brooks Brother is a *Playa* who knows the power of an attractive image. This image reels in a lot of women, but what lies beneath that exterior is a master manipulator, con man and serial cheater most women will ultimately run from.

FLIPPING THE GAME

How do you flip the game on *The Brooks Brother*?

An arrogant man is the easiest man to play! Most *Brooks Brothers* are arrogant *Playas*. They've been playing women for so long without getting caught or checked, that they believe women are stupid. That attitude makes it easy for women to flip the game on them.

Get over on this *Playa* while he's trying to impress you with expensive dinners and bottles of $100 champagne during the first few dates.

Steer him to the most expensive restaurants in town. Act like you've been to those places with other men a dozen times (even if you haven't) so that he feels pressure to live up to that image.

Tell him you want to get your hair and nails done to look good for him. Ask him to pay your gym membership for a year.

Drain this Playboy financially within the first few weeks of knowing him. His money will run out soon after that and he'll then be looking to flip the script and game you.

Make him pay to play. By the time he realizes you've played him, you're on your way to the next…

THE MARRIED PLAYA

Some men continue to play women even when they marry, commit to or, start living with one woman. These unavailable Playboys need the excitement of dating multiple women to feel alive. They also feed off of the drama that having more than one woman creates.

The Married Playa is that guy! He is not content unless he has women competing for his attention and vying for his affection. *The Married Playa* enjoys the stability and comfort of having a wife at home…but he is happiest when there is at least one other woman in his life.

The Married Playa seeks out women who will not interfere with his happy home, women who will understand his situation and sympathize with his circumstances. He wants a woman he can control emotionally, mentally and sexually—someone so desperate for a man that she will accept having a piece of man rather than go without having one at all.

HOW CAN YOU SPOT THE MARRIED PLAYA?

The Married Playa's game is always the same. He creates a cover story that is saleable to women. This cover allows *The Married Playa* to (1) paint himself as a victim and (2) justify his cheating ways.

In most cases *The Married Playa* will tell the women he's pursuing that he's married to a monster. He will claim his home life is hell and that he wants out but cannot get out for some reason. He will claim his wife is crazy -- bi-polar, an alcoholic, depressed, etc. – anything to paint himself as a victim:

"I'm just waiting for the kids to graduate…" *The Married Playa* claims.

"My wife is sick. I can't leave her now, but the marriage is over."

"I don't love my wife anymore. She's too (fat, mean, demanding, controlling, etc.)"

"If I leave now, she'll take the kids and I won't see them again."

The Married Playa needs to draw women into his personal drama. He needs to paint himself as the victim of pathetic circumstance. He needs the mistress to believe he's looking for a way out. More importantly, he needs her to take his side and believe that she is better (in some way) than his wife.

This emotional game causes the side woman to compete for *The Married Playa*. She turns her life upside down trying to keep her married lover happy and get him to leave his 'unhappy home'.

What happens in most cases however, is just the opposite. *The Married Playa* delays moving out or getting a divorce again and again. No matter what the mistress does, *The Married Playa* stays put. He doesn't leave his 'psycho wife' or his comfortable home. In fact, he never had any real intentions of leaving his wife, and the only way he'll get a divorce is if she files the paperwork and serves him.

The Married Playa's game is as old as time:

SELL A SUCKER A DREAM!

Most of us know at least one friend who has been a sucker for a married man. So many women fall for *The Married Playa's* weak game:

"Baby, if I knew you before I met my wife, I would have married you in a heartbeat."

"I only married her because she got pregnant. I don't love her like I love you."

Many women hearing statements like the above will buy into that fantasy and will start planning a life with a man who could never be hers. She will start telling friends that her married lover <u>WILL</u> LEAVE his wife. She's sure of it.

"He told me he doesn't love her anymore" the mistress insists. *"He's going to leave her…"*

To play you, *The Married Playa* only needs you to believe in a dream!

"One day baby…one day we'll be together!"

"You're the woman I really want/need."

The question women who are dealing with married men should ask themselves is this:

IF LIFE IS SO BAD WITH HER AND YOU THINK 'I'M ALL THAT', WHY ARE YOU STILL WITH YOUR WIFE AND NOT ME?

The truth is,

HE'S NOT WITH YOU BECAUSE HE'D RATHER BE WITH HER.

PEEP GAME

People leave relationships when they are ready. If they aren't ready to leave, they will give themselves (and you) a thousand reasons why they have to stay.

THE BOTTOM LINE

If a man is married to a woman, she is the woman he wants to be with. Unless he files for divorce and then moves out of the marital home…know that he is lying when he says he'd rather be with you.

MORE CHARACTERISTICS AND TACTICS OF THE MARRIED PLAYBOY:

- He tends to work the type of job or work schedule that keeps him out of town or on the move. He can't be pinned down at an office and there is no one you can call but him to confirm his whereabouts. If given a choice of fixed hours or a flexible schedule, he will choose the latter.

- He chooses jobs that keep him around a lot of women and he revels in the attention these women give him.

- He has several female friends. They call him regularly for advice and general conversation.

- He's obsessed with staying fit and looking good.

- He tells the women he's pursuing what time he will be available to meet and/or talk, and he expects them to talk to and meet him at those times.

- He says he lives with a roommate or with a relative and can't invite you over because (they get up early, are on bad terms, etc.)

- One minute he's not available for days at a time, the next minute he's practically living with you for a week.

- His clothes are perfectly matched…too perfectly matched.

- He cleans up before going home.

- He only introduces you to 1 of his friends or refuses to introduce you to his family.

- His child is under 1 years old.

- His friends barely acknowledge you. They are dismissive and act like you don't exist.

The Married Playa uses his work schedule or profession to explain absences and to allow himself more time and opportunities to play.

He often seduces women at work, at church or other places where their behavior will be constrained.

He likes to see women fight over him and may instigate arguments between his main woman and mistress.

FLIPPING THE GAME

How do you flip the game on *The Married Playa*?

You can't. There is no upside to being #2 or 1 of 2. No matter how you slice it, dealing with a cheating lover is a losing proposition. Why deal with a man who can't commit when there are so many other available men who are looking for a woman like you?

THE INTERNATIONAL PLAYA

A friend of mine visited Africa. At one of the hotels she stayed at, she met a beautiful dark-skinned man with the kind of body you see on the covers of fitness magazines. This man was a tour guide for American tourists. It was his job to show travelers around town.

My friend called me from Africa to tell me about this wonderful new guy she'd met.

"He is so sweet" she mused.

"He is treating me like a queen."

I listened dutifully like a good friend is supposed to, but I had my doubts about the guy. After all, my friend traveled to Africa with a group of well-to-do African-Americans who all paid good money to tour the mother country in style. It would look to the hotel employees servicing them, like my friend was well-off, even though her trip was paid for by a relative.

Add in the fact that my friend was the type to fall hard and fast – the type who asked no questions up front and learned everything about the men in her life the hard way.

This was a recipe for failure…but I kept my mouth shut and congratulated my friend on meeting who she believed was "the one."

Days later my friend returned home and immediately started sending money to her new African boyfriend.

"He needs things," she would tell me. "His job doesn't pay much."

Again, I said nothing.

She sent money a few times more times but then *Playa, Playa* started asking for specific amounts of money. He also expressed his desire to move to America and claimed to need a few thousand dollars to get the process started.

After hearing about this guy for a few months, it was clear to me that he was running game. This *International Playboy* was using my friend to supplement his income and live the high life in Africa. He had no intentions of coming to America. He only said that because he knew that's what she wanted to hear.

I tried to tell my friend then, that she was dealing with a *Playa*. I tried to tell her that he was probably running this same con on at least one woman from every bus load of tourists that passed through his town. I tried to tell her that she was being used…

You know she didn't listen. You also probably know what happened next.

After a few months of talking to this guy for hours at a time and sending him thousands of dollars via Western Union, the African stopped answering my friend's calls. Through letters he started claiming the other hotel workers weren't giving him messages and that he had to work more hours so he had little free time to chat.

Eventually, communication stopped completely.

I then had to answer the question "Why" for my friend? She was ready to hear what I'd tried to tell her all along.

This is what I told her:

"The game is the same, only the Playas are different. He wanted your money. When he saw that you couldn't/wouldn't send him the amount of money he wanted on a consistent basis, he cut you off and moved on to a bigger fish."

Another friend of mine went through a similar situation with an *International Playa.* He courted my friend by phone long distance. He convinced her to marry him so that he could gain citizenship. He promised to be with her when he arrived in America. She sent thousands of dollars to him to cover his relocation expenses.

Weeks after arriving in the United States, homeboy disappeared. My friend was stuck in a marriage with a man she couldn't find.

I remember her calling me desperate to find him before a certain date so that she could annul the marriage. Three years later, this man who claimed he knew no one in the U.S was still M.I.A. *The Playa* had literally taken her money and ran!

THE BOTTOM LINE

The International Playa targets women who are lonely and desperate to get married. He can smell their thirst a mile away. He spins a tale and sells her a dream so that he can get what he wants from her.

Like a farmer drawing water from a well, *The International Playa* works a well until it runs dry.

If he suspects his target woman is getting wise to his game or she slows up on sending him Money Grams, *The International Playa* will end communication and move on!

Just like *The Hard Luck Playa*, *The International Playa* wants money. He'll give you a sob story – a 'Down on My Luck' tale.

He wants you to sponsor his lifestyle. Know that he will stick around only as long as you can supply him with ends.

FLIPPING THE GAME

How do you flip the game on *The International Playa*?

The best way to flip the game on an International Playboy is to become an International Playgirl. Instead of sending your new lover gifts from your homeland, ask him to send you gifts from his. Tell him you really miss the sunset from _____ beach and would really love it if he could send you a framed piece of art depicting that location. Ask him to send you clothing/jewelry from his country. Ask him to send you a gift basket of chocolates from a local but famed chocolatier in his city.

Keep this guy jumping through hoops. See how far he's willing to stretch his pockets. The only way to gage a man's interest in you is to see how far he is willing to go FOR YOU!!!

THE JAIL BIRD

The Jail Bird is another type of *Hard Luck Playa*! This guy uses his bad situation (being in jail or facing time) to game women and get money from them.

A lot of women don't think men who have nothing (including their freedom) can effectively run game on women. But that is a LIE! Men in prison are arguably THE MOST cunning men on the planet.

Many of them know nothing but how to hustle people. They depend on conning, manipulating and cheating to meet their daily needs.

They have spent years honing their conversation skills, persuasion techniques, thievery and poker face. Not only that, their traumatic and unstable childhoods taught them how NOT to care about another person's feelings.

If there is any playa in this book who should be considered the *Grand Don* of *Mackin',* it would be *The Jailbird*.

Ladies…peep game!

HOW DO YOU SPOT THE JAIL BIRD PLAYBOY?

Here is a list of *his* patterns and tactics:

- **He will never admit to the crime he is accused of committing.** He will insist someone else did the crime and that he was in the wrong place at the wrong time or, set up.

  The Jail Bird will never tell the truth about his crimes because that would be out of character for this cunning Playboy.. This guy's whole existence is based on lies. Additionally, playing the victim ensures that you (and his unconditionally loving mother) will support him financially and emotionally through years of hard time.

- **He keeps a side chick or ties to old girlfriends.** Many *Jail Birds* pursue and maintain relationships with more than one woman while in prison. These men need money on their books every week for commissary. They need someone to call. They may need someone on the outside to run errands. And they definitely need someone to pay lawyers and/or their bail.

The Jail Bird has a lot of expenses and a lifestyle to maintain. He knows that in order to keep his commissary account full and his other needs fulfilled, he will need more than one gullible female to call on.

- **He writes the most romantic letters when he's locked up.** Your boyfriend never gives you cards and he's definitely not a poet, but since going to prison, you are now getting the most romantic letters and cards.

  Many Jail Birds employ men in prison to write letters and cards. In exchange for a few packs of coffee, your boyfriend gets a long, sappy letter that you will love.. Before you run around the office with that beautiful 10 page letter from your 'innocent but jailed baby daddy', know that he probably didn't write it.

- **He promises to change…**
  Your first love goes to prison on a 3 year bid. He asks you to remain loyal because when he gets out, he's going to change his life around. He promises

to go back to school, get a job, take care of you, etc. It all sounds good but...

The reality is this: Your boyfriend is merely telling you what he knows you want to hear. Every Jail Bird knows the women in their lives want to hear that they've changed. They also know that in order to get support from mom, sis, girlfriend, baby mama...they have to pretend to be a changed man.

Many convicts will assume a cover personality during visits with you and in letters...all in an effort to con you out of time, energy and MONEY.

This guy has no intention of changing his ways, but in order to keep you around, he'll say whatever he needs to.

THE BOTTOM LINE

The biggest issue for women who date incarcerated Playboys is the fact that they waste YEARS on a man who is not ready, willing or able to change. These men prey on rescuer type women who need someone to cheerlead and take care of. The sad part is, when many of these *Playas* get out of jail, they break up with the Ride or Die Chick who did time with them, choosing instead to go solo or pursue a relationship with someone new.

Peep Game

The thug you think has changed his ways…

The hustler you could never pin down but who now calls 2-3 times a day just to see how you're doing…

The cheater who kept you on an emotional rollercoaster, but now seems to have learned his lesson…

IS PLAYING YOU!

His game is persuasion – getting you to do what he needs done while he's locked up. Everything this man says is script – a carefully spun web of lies. He is not a changed man. He is only one pretending to be!

A friend of mine once told me she was done messing with men in jail. She had been played for the last time!

She told me about her baby daddy, who would go in and out of prison. She would visit him regularly as well as keep money on his books.

This guy was supposedly a pretty boy. He was allegedly fine as cat hair – the type of guy women swoon over. Not surprisingly, he had multiple women and kept my friend on an emotional wreck when he was 'out.'

Nevertheless, my friend supported the guy every time he went to prison because he always claimed he'd learned his lesson and was committed to change.

One day she visited him in prison. As she headed out of the visitation room, she spots one of the women her baby daddy used to mess with on the side entering the room. She then realized that her CHANGED baby's father was playing her.

He had her, his side chick and probably many others visiting him, calling him, and putting money on his books.

She told me she felt like the biggest fool because she'd spent thousands of dollars she couldn't afford on a man who was only pretending to want her and to change.

My friend's story is just one woman's tale of dealing with a *Jail Bird Playboy*. Unfortunately, her experience is not unusual or unheard of.

FLIPPING THE GAME

How do you flip the game on *The Jail Bird*?

If you're dating a man who is committing crimes, you have to prepare for the day when he will get caught. While the money is rolling in, however, you need to set yourself up financially so that you can easily weather that storm.

Instead of waiting for the shoe to drop (aka the feds to roll in and take everything), and then trying to collect money all over town...tell your boyfriend to give you an allowance. Get a piece of that pie!

Take this money and separate out a portion for living on, a portion for saving, and a portion to invest in a business/career/education.

Don't tell your guy what you're doing. He'll just insist you bring that money down to the jailhouse (when he gets arrested) and use it to pay his bail or a lawyer. Keep this money hidden in a separate account that no one knows exists but you.

Also, insist that your man get life insurance, and if you two are engaged, married, living together or raising children, make sure you are the beneficiary. Make sure the policy is at least $50,000. (He can set up another policy for his mother if he wants her taken care of too)

If *The Jail Bird* dies, you and mom can pay for a lovely funeral and burial, plus you'll still have money left over to pay off some bills or move forward in your own life.

THE WEB BROWSER

Thanks to social media and the popularity of online dating sites, men are able to play women through a computer screen.

A *Playa* in Africa sitting at an Internet café can pretend to be a London business man. A Playboy living in Mississippi can pretend to be a popular Las Vegas party promoter. A married reverend can pretend to be single and available.

The Internet is the modern Playboy's most useful tool for gaming and taming women. Men who use the Internet to lure and run game on women are *Web Browsers*. These men troll social networks and dating sites looking for women they can bump and dump, use and abuse, manipulate and control.

The Web Browser is usually a man who is looking for easy sex. He is looking for a hook-up, someone he can see casually every now and then or for one night of freaky sex. Some *Web Browser's* however, are scam artists who want money from their targets, not a sexual encounter.

HOW CAN YOU SPOT THE WEB BROWSER?

- His profile looks and sounds too good to be true. *"I'm six-foot-two with an athletic build" his profile reads. "I love snowboarding and international travel. I'm looking for a good woman who is ready for commitment."* If someone sounds too good to be true, they probably are.

- His contact number is a work phone or a cell phone that is never answered.

- He has no activity on his timeline. He either just started his page (SUSPECT) or has all of his activity hidden (EVEN MORE SUSPECT).
- While chatting online, he mentions that he has a roommate. (This tactic – often used by married men - is supposed to explain his inability to bring you to his place or his desire to talk/chat ONLY during business hours)

- He wants to meet the same night you respond to his friend request/follow/flirty message.

- He says he lives with his mother. (Another tactic used by married men who don't want you asking to visit them at home).

- When you call, he texts back.

- He's available at the same times every day. He never posts after 6 pm and doesn't respond to messages on the weekend.

- He's chatted with, met or had sex with other women on your friend list.

- He never posts things publicly but constantly sends you private messages.
- He asks for money or hints that he needs money during the first few communications.

- He asks for sex or hints that you are probably good in bed during the first few communications.

- He sends you a d*ck pic without asking you first or, tells you how big his penis is. (HE'S TESTING THE WATERS)

- He asks you to send him a picture of your breasts, butt or vagina. (AGAIN HE'S GAGING YOUR GULLIBILITY)

- The first date offline is at your house or his. He didn't want to go anywhere, just chill with you.

- You Google what he says is his real name and nothing comes up.

- You Google what he claims is his address and are pointed to something like a post office or a tree.

- You ask him about the city he supposedly lives in and he only tells you things that everybody knows about that city.

  "Oh, I love to visit the Skydeck at the Willis Tower in Chicago."

  No Chicagoan who has lived in the city for more than a few years would say that. Something like, *"I'd love to take you to 'Andies' in Andersonville. They have great Mediterranean food"* indicates a man actually knows/lives in Chicago.

THE BOTTOM LINE

The Web Browser uses the Internet to hunt for naïve, gullible women. He has a lot of profiles on several social networks and dating sites. He is looking for women who will give him (without resistance) sex or the money in her bank account.

The Web Browser attracts a lot of women thanks to a dynamic profile, complete with a old picture of him, a photo of an attractive relative or, a handsome stranger.

He has bait words weaved into the "Who Am I?" section of his profile.

Words like…

"Good Man"

"Hard-Working"

"Gentleman"

"Father"

"Christian"

"Loyal Friend"

…he knows, will get women to pay attention to him.

If a profile looks too good to be true, it probably is!

MORE PATTERNS AND TACTICS OF THE WEB BROWSER:

- **His phone voice doesn't match the wording he uses online.**

  People speak the way that they write. A person's personality, culture, age and gender are evident in the way that they write. A guy from Brooklyn, New York will use certain phrases common to New York. An African guy living in London will have completely different phrasing and vernacular. If you've been chatting with someone online but you find that they speak totally different than they write…you could be dealing with a Playa who is using "copy" (aka scripted text) to bait you.

- **He tells you he's in need!**

  Men who are Playas rarely waste time with women who are not ripe for the picking. They don't have the time or energy to talk a woman into having sex with them or giving them money. They'd rather work on a mark who is ripe.

  If you're talking/chatting with a man who gets straight to the point like, "Hey, can I meet you now?" or "I'm a little short on rent this month; can you help me out?" you're probably dealing with a playa.

- **He's name dropping.**

  In order to convince you that you're dealing with a winner, The Web Browser may pretend to be a bigger deal than he really is. Some will name drop celebrities or musicians. Some will claim to know Warren Buffett or the head of Boeing. If a man is dropping names like crazy, he's probably lying about his connections. He is also more than likely priming you for some good game.

- **He shows up in a car different from the one he claims to drive every day.**

  The Web Browser will claim his cousin needed the Benz for the night or that he caught a flat at the last minute and borrowed his roommate's Ford Focus.

  He promises to pick you up in the Corvette next time...the Bentley as soon as the front end is fixed. This is all game. Any man who drives a luxury car like a Benz or a Bentley has insurance that will pay for a comparable rental.

- **He offers to make you dinner!**

  You think it's cute that your Web Browser wants to make you dinner for the first date. The truth is, this

Playa is looking for a way into your house so that he can smash and pass.

Years ago I was chatting with this guy who was pursuing me online. He told me (and I confirmed) that he was taking master's classes at a local university. He really seemed like a great catch. After talking on the phone a time or two, this *Web Browser* asked if we could meet. I gave him a couple days and times I'd be available and suggested we meet at a coffee house near my home.

He gave the oddest answer I've ever heard. He said he got paid a week after the dates I'd given and wouldn't have any money to spend on a big date.

"Can I come over and make you dinner instead" he asked?

I told him "No!"

I cook pretty well myself and didn't need or want a stranger cooking anything for me in my home.

He insisted on cooking something…anything I wanted.

I asked him how he would buy the food for dinner if he was broke until payday. He told me he could bring a bottle of $8 *Andre* champagne or a pint of liquor if I preferred.

"I can make anything you have in the fridge," he said with pride.

I said this before hanging up the phone and blocking him online...

"I don't need any man to cook the food in my refrigerator for me. How about we talk after payday?"

This *Web Browser* appeared to be a good catch. He had a job, was finishing his master's degree and spoke intelligently. The reality however, was very different.

FLIPPING THE GAME

How do you flip the game on *The Web Browser*?

Google everything this guy tells you about him. Put his name, supposed address, workplace…everything in Google Search. See what comes up! Do this as you guys are talking or chatting. Say nothing about it. Just open a new tab on your phone/tablet, and in between messages, search the information he gives you.

If you come across a discrepancy, confront *The Web Browser* about it.

"You said you worked at 920 Parkers Way? That's a gas station not a bank."

Watch him squirm and try to lie his way out of that mess

The way you flip the game on *The Web Browser* is by peeping game. In this way, you avoid wasting time and energy on a man who is running game.

FINAL THOUGHTS

Men who are *Playas* are well-practiced and well-rehearsed. They seem to know exactly what to say and exactly what to do in every situation with women.

They have an answer for everything!

They are smooth talkers and are calmly assertive.

Not much you say or do gets them angry so most often they respond to conflict and drama with a chuckle and a smile or a dismissive wave. (Red flag)

The *Playa* knows how to play the game, and that includes knowing how to talk his way into and out of any situation with women. He is a con artist and his con of choice is running GAME on women.

YOU CAN TELL A PLAYA FROM A REGULAR CAT

If you pay attention, you'll notice the differences between guys who are not *Playas* and guys who are. Guys who are not *Playas*, are less rehearsed, more spontaneous, and often clumsy in their approach to women.

For example:

You're standing at the bus stop and a guy approaches you. We'll call him Abe. Abe is fine as all get out and as he saunters up to you, you're squealing inside from the delight of knowing Abe is headed straight for you. Abe approaches you and then opens his mouth to speak.

He mumbles something like, *"Hey! You look like my sister's friend Carmella."*

You look at him like he's crazy. *"What?"*

Abe tries again. *"I mean, I want to say, I think you're very pretty."*

Your heart sinks because what you thought would be a great connection with a hot new guy just went bust. Abe is cute but he can't seem to get his words together. He's asking you random questions and sounds like the biggest goof. By the time he gets around to asking for your number, your bus has arrived. You make a run for it, glad to get away from goofy Abe.

A few days later you're standing at the same bus stop. A nice looking guy slides by in a beautiful Chrysler 300.

We'll call him Cam. He eyes you up and down and shoots a *"Hello"* through the window. You wave back.

You think, *"This is the kind of guy I like."*

Lucky for you Cam is headed to the drugstore you're standing in front of. He parks his car and then saunters up to you from behind. *"Hey baby girl. What you doing standing out here all by yourself?"*

You turn around and take Cam in…all 6 ft. 3 inch 225 lbs. of him. He looks good, smells good and sounds even better. Within minutes he's gotten your number, your zodiac sign, your height, weight, and shoe size. As he walks away, you program Cam into your phone's calendar for Friday night. He's already asked you to reserve the date.

5 minutes later your phone rings. It's Cam. *"Just checking ma. Making sure this is you. Have a good day!"*

You practically skip onto the bus you're so happy.

By now you should have guessed which one of these guys is a *Playa*. It's guy #2.

While guy #1 (Abe) is just as cute and just as interested in the girl at the bus stop as guy #2 appears to be, only Abe really wants to get to know the girl at the bus stop.

Cam is a *Playa*. He's looking for a Drive-by, a Booty Call, a Side-Chick or (what we call in the Chi)…a Dip.

Abe is so nervous that he stutters and stumbles in his attempt to initiate conversation. This indicates he's not a PRO at approaching women. He's in unfamiliar territory, and that can be a good thing.

On the other hand, Cam is so comfortable approaching women he can initiate a conversation and get a woman's contact information within minutes without even thinking about it. He knows exactly what to say to women to get them to focus on what he's saying. He knows how to get women into him. His conversation is well-rehearsed. Cam is a ladies man, and he's running what *Playas* call "a script."

The point is ladies, a guy who is a *Playa* is usually a smooth talker and a smooth operator. He leaves nothing (or very little) to chance. He has a modus operandi that is used so frequently it looks and sounds like script. Remember that!

A Playa's M.O. will look and sound like a script!

- *The Playa* has certain restaurants he'll want to go to. (He doesn't care what you like to eat. He won't even ask). He has a list of restaurants he takes EVERY girl to.

Modus Operandi.

- He has a stash of condoms in his glove compartment. He has a fresh work shirt with a toothbrush and bottle of cologne in the trunk of his car just in case he spends the night out unexpectedly.

Modus Operandi.

On the other hand, the regular guy is not as prepared.

- He will not have fresh condoms in the glove box. If he does, they've expired and are no good. It's been that long…

- When you guys decide to meet for dinner he will have to google a restaurant or ask you for a suggestion on where to eat. After all, he's not out every Friday, Saturday and Sunday with a new chick.

Plus, he cares about your preferences. *"Let's go to one of your favorite restaurants."*

- If he stays the night, he may have to rush home first thing in the morning to shower and get a fresh shirt. He's ill-prepared and un-rehearsed.

Many women think the Average Joe's clumsy approach means he's a square. Then they look at the smooth operating *Playa* and call him "on point." The truth is this: You want a man to be clumsy. You want him to be a bit unsure. You want him to be ill-prepared for sex. These are signs that he's not with a new chick every week.

* * * *

So many women get played every day of the year because they don't know what to look for while dating. The warning signs a man is,

- A habitual cheater
- A pathological liar
- A manipulator
- A con artist

…are right in front of women, but they ignore these obvious traits.

I don't blame these women for their poor dating choices. You know what you know. The thing is, once you learn how the game is played, there is no excuse for letting men who are *Playas* get over on you.

I have just given you a complete guide to the liars, con artists and manipulators of the dating game. I have revealed every trick of their trade. You, beautiful lady, have just been given the tools you need to "PEEP GAME"

Use this book to protect your heart—to avoid the misery of repeated heartache and pain. Remember, you've got to make it to the other side. You've got to stay fly and fabulous for your prince…

That said, don't let this information sit on your bookshelf. Pull this book out every so often so that your game stays tight.

And finally, now that you know the game…I ask you to do one thing for me. Pass this knowledge on!

Each one teach one is my motto.

Don't hate the Playas ladies, learn how the game is played!

ABOUT BUTTA 'FLY' JONEZ

In August 2010, I launched a website for women called "Peep Game." That website covered topics I felt weren't being covered accurately or sufficiently by other dating blogs and books. Topics like "How to Get a Man to Give You What You Want," "How to Get Money From Men," "Married in 365" and "Always The Baby Mama, Never The Bride" delved into subjects and shared information that women really wanted and needed to know and understand about dating.

After publishing articles for 4 years, I decided to transform the most popular blogs from "Peep Game" into useful dating guides.

My first books covered the topics "How to Be a Female Player" and dating rich (see the following page). "How to Spot a Playa" is my 5th dating guide, but there is so much more to come.

I plan to follow this book up with books "Act Like a Lady, Think Like a Mack" and "8 Types of Men and How to Play Them."

To me it's about leveling the playing field! I want women to be as informed and empowered as many men are about how to date strategically and efficiently.

I am not against men or even how men play the game. I believe dating is a game. I believe, those with the knowledge of how to play come out on top (aka win).

Success in dating is as simple as learning how men think, how they approach the game as well as effective strategies for getting what you want out of your relationships with men.

It's not about playing the fool or being a perpetual victim. Learn how the game is played and create the dating experiences you want and deserve!

I can help you do that.

Much Love,

Butta 'Fly' Jonez

OTHER BOOKS BY BUTTA 'FLY' JONEZ

How to be a Female Player

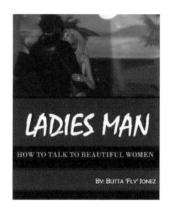

How to Talk to Beautiful Women

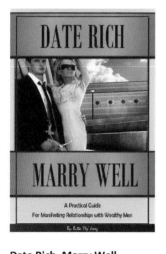

Date Rich, Marry Well

I AM BEAUTIFUL

Printed in Great Britain
by Amazon